Lies About Truth And The Truth About Lies

By Pastor Bill Jenkins

Lies About Truth
And The
Truth About Lies

By Pastor Bill Jenkins

Manufactured in the
United States of America
ISBN # 979-8-218-16347-1

Published by
B&B Media
Upland, California
Visit the author's website at:
www.pastorbilljenkins.org

TABLE OF CONTENTS

INTRODUCTION

Before I write one word or you read one page of this book, everyone already knows you should never tell a lie and that you should always tell the truth. We do not need another book to tell us what we already know we have to do. Lying is wrong and telling the truth is always the best policy. We have heard it from our childhood, and we preach it as adults. We all know the difference between the truth and a lie, but the reason I am even writing this book is to help give us the encouragement to walk out the truth even when it is easier to lie. Personally, I hate lying even though I have lied and have made a commitment to always speak the truth. It is not always that easy. Lying is destructive. Telling the truth is liberating even when there are consequences attached to telling the truth. We have to establish truth as a way of life in every part of our lives. Speaking the truth and walking out the truth can never be optional. It must be a personal decision that is rooted from the integrity that comes from within our hearts. Truth comes from being connected with Jesus Christ and applying the knowledge we get from God's Holy Word. Jesus is truth and Jesus is the Word of God. We can never have truth outside God and the scriptures. Truth is the only way to expose darkness and walk in the light.

- Telling the truth builds trust with others.
- Telling the truth brings peace of mind.
- Telling the truth is being true to yourself.
- Telling the truth is required for a connection with God.

This book is written out of my study and messages that I have preached to congregations throughout the years, but more importantly it is birthed from a heart that seeks to be always motivated by the truth. This is not some book of personal opinions or helpful suggestions. It is a book of commands that is based on the absolute truth of the Word of God. Like it or not, take it or leave it, this book is what it is. It is an in-depth look at everything you ever wanted to know or even did not want to know about truth and lies. You may not be able to handle a book like this right now at this time in your life but keep it handy because when you are ready for the truth this book is for you. I am putting verbs in my sentences and drawing a clear line between truth and lies. Ultimately it is your choice, but my prayer is that we always seek truth over lies every day of our lives. To sum everything up, the truth about lies is that the truth never lies and the lie about the truth is that lies never tell the truth. Your desire to read this book and apply the truth says a lot about who you really are …

"We are from God, and whoever knows God listens to us; but whoever is not from God does not listen to us. This is how we recognize the Spirit of truth and the spirit of falsehood."
1 John 4:6 NIV

We all must make a personal decision to be honest or deceptive. We must take a stand and draw a line in the sand, when it comes to premeditating the truth. It should not be an option for the child of God when it comes to what side of the line you are going to choose. My hope is that the words you read in this book will convict and motivate you to always be truthful regardless of what comes your way in life. Honesty is always the best policy, so choose truth and choose life.

The first lie the devil will tell you is against the last truth God speaks

CHAPTER 1
WHAT IS A LIE?

A lie is simply defined as an assertation or statement that is untrue, inaccurate, or incomplete. Lies are words intended to mislead or deceive another person. Lying was the first sin introduced into the world by Satan in the Garden.

"Now the serpent was more subtil than any beast of the field which the Lord God had made. And he said unto the woman, Yea, hath God said, Ye shall not eat of every tree of the garden?" Genesis 3:1

God never said that Adam and Eve could not eat from every tree of the garden, just one tree. Yet the enemy used partial truth to attempt to deceive them. However, even Eve knew it was a lie when she responded negatively to the devil's deception in verses 2 and 3.

"And the woman said unto the serpent, We may eat of the fruit of the trees of the garden: But of the fruit of the tree which is in the midst of the garden, God hath said, Ye shall not eat of it, neither shall ye touch it, lest ye die." Genesis 3:2-3

She responded almost 100% correct but failed in her last words by saying, "shall not touch" and "lest ye die." God never said they could not touch it. He only said they would die if they ate it. Eve added to the words of God. By conversing with the enemy, she was falling into a trap that would cause her thinking to be twisted and her mind to be open to deception. Two facts to already remember when figuring out the truth from the lie is:

1. Lying is always contrary to the nature of God.

   "Jesus saith unto him, I am the way, the truth, and the life: no man cometh unto the Father, but by me." John 14:6

2. Lying is always complimentary to the nature of the devil.

   "Ye are of your father the devil, and the lusts of your father ye will do. He was a murderer from the beginning, and abode not in the truth, because there is no truth in him. When he speaketh a lie, he speaketh of his own: for he is a liar, and the father of it." John 8:44

When I speak of someone's nature, I refer to who someone is, not just what someone does. God does not just speak Truth, He is Truth. The devil does not just speak lies, he is a Liar.

Lying is subtle and always done with deceit. There are various kinds of lies and types of liars.

Three Types of Liars

1. Liars by Intention

    An intentional lie is a lie without an excuse or reason. They lie on purpose and lie about things that are unnecessary. They are habitual liars whose intent is to mislead and deceive others.

2. Liars by Insinuation

    Notice how even the word insinuation includes the word "sin." Insinuating is implying something so that someone concludes an untruth. Insinuating is a subtle suggestion in an indirect way designed to mislead others. It is an art that only professional liars have mastered.

3. Liars by Incompleteness

    An incomplete lie is a half-truth, and half-truths are whole lies. Half-truths leave a false impression concerning a matter when the whole truth could bring clarity. Whenever there are two sides to a story, there are always three conclusions: your side, their side, and the truth.

Lying also has many different characteristics to help you identify it for what it is.

Seven Characteristics of Lying

1. Flattery

   "A lying tongue hateth those that are afflicted by it; and a flattering mouth worketh ruin." Proverbs 26:28

   There is a difference between a genuine compliment and the manipulation of flattery. Compliments are selfless and based on truth. Flattery is selfish and designed to manipulate gullible people. Flattery can definitely be a form of lying.

2. Slanderers

   "He that hideth hatred with lying lips, and he that uttereth a slander, is a fool." Proverbs 10:18

   A slanderer is a person who attempts to damage another's reputation. Making false charges or misrepresenting someone's reputation is not just wrong, it is a lie.

3. Exaggeration

"Wherefore putting away lying, speak every man truth with his neighbour: for we are members one of another." *Ephesians 4:25*

Be careful not to sensationalize the facts. Be accurate in calculating numbers because exaggerating the truth is a lie.

4. Gossipers

"He that goeth about as a talebearer revealeth secrets: therefore meddle not with him that flattereth with his lips." *Proverbs 20:19*

A gossiper spreads rumors and not facts. They are nosey people who cannot mind their own business. They are delivering the devil's mail. They are the devil's postman, and they are liars.

5. Superstitious

"But refuse profane and old wives' fables and exercise thyself rather unto godliness." *1 Timothy 4:7*

Superstition is defined as an ignorant and irrational belief or practice. It is a trust in a human formula or magical ceremony. All superstitious acts are the devil's way to deceive and lie.

6. False Teachers

"O Timothy, keep that which is committed to thy trust, avoiding profane and vain babblings, and oppositions of science falsely so called:" 1 Timothy 6:20

There are false teachers who will water down the scripture and pet your devils by not declaring the convicting Word of God. Anyone who adds to the Word of God or takes something away from the Word of God, should be avoided because they are a liar.

7. Hypocrites

"And why call ye me, Lord, Lord, and do not the things which I say?" Luke 6:46

A hypocrite is someone who puts on a mask and pretends to be something they are not. They are actors who say one thing but do not match their actions with their words. They are liars.

Exaggeration is at

least a cousin

of a lie

A lie can be by omission or commission. It can be committed unintentionally, or it can be done purposely by omitting something from a story. Either way, it is a lie. There are a lot of ways to achieve a lie and there are a lot of ways to deceive others. In many ways, lying is about the character of an individual. It is about the heart of what is inside someone. Deceiving others is easy, but accepting our own deception is another level of evil. Do not be tolerant of the evil of lying. Be conscious of what you are saying and always think before you speak. Carefully craft your words to present the truth to others.

When you really want to pursue the truth, lying becomes clearer than ever. As Christians we must not just avoid lying. We must also seek the truth that comes only from God's Holy Word. Lying was not only the first sin introduced to mankind, but it is also one the of the last things mentioned in the Bible.

> *"For without are dogs, and sorcerers, and whoremongers, and murderers, and idolaters, and whosoever loveth and maketh a lie." Revelation 22:15*

Lying not only offends, but it also separates us from God. It does not just have the ability to separate us temporarily but also for eternity. Avoid lying and walk in the truth.

The Bible says a liar is:

- Insane

  "As a mad man who casteth firebrands, arrows, and death, So is the man that deceiveth his neighbour, and saith, Am not I in sport?" Proverbs 26:18-19

- Deceitful

  "He that worketh deceit shall not dwell within my house: he that telleth lies shall not tarry in my sight." Psalm 101:7

- A Murderer

  "Woe to the bloody city! it is all full of lies and robbery; the prey departeth not;" Nahum 3:1

- Cowardly

  "But the fearful, and unbelieving, and the abominable, and murderers, and whoremongers, and sorcerers, and idolaters, and all liars, shall have their part in the lake which burneth with fire and brimstone: which is the second death." Revelation 21:8

- Selfish

  "But if ye have bitter envying and strife in your hearts, glory not, and lie not against the truth." James 3:14

- Hated

  "A lying tongue hateth those that are afflicted by it; and a flattering mouth worketh ruin." Proverbs 26:28

- Foolish

  "Excellent speech becometh not a fool: much less do lying lips a prince." Proverbs 17:7

- A False Prophet

  "Beware of false prophets, which come to you in sheep's clothing, but inwardly they are ravening wolves." Matthew 7:15

- Denied Eternal Life

  "But the fearful, and unbelieving, and the abominable, and murderers, and whoremongers, and sorcerers, and idolaters, and all liars, shall have their part in the lake which burneth with fire

and brimstone: which is the second death." Revelation 21:8

- A Blasphemer

"Ye shall not steal, neither deal falsely, neither lie one to another. And ye shall not swear by my name falsely, neither shalt thou profane the name of thy God: I am the Lord." Leviticus 19:11-12

- A Divider

"Now I beseech you, brethren, mark them which cause divisions and offences contrary to the doctrine which ye have learned; and avoid them. For they that are such serve not our Lord Jesus Christ, but their own belly; and by good words and fair speeches deceive the hearts of the simple." Romans 16:17-18

- A Scoundrel

"The instruments also of the churl are evil: he deviseth wicked devices to destroy the poor with lying words, even when the needy speaketh right." Isaiah 32:7

Lying to yourself and others is like jumping out of a perfectly good plane without a parachute. It is destructive and deadly. Lying leads to darkness and death, but the truth leads to light and life.

CHAPTER 2
THE TRUTH ABOUT LIES

To be honest and to get right to the point, people lie because we are inherently evil.

"For there is not a just man upon earth, that doeth good, and sinneth not." Ecclesiastes 7:20

"For all have sinned, and come short of the glory of God;" Romans 3:23

"The heart is deceitful above all things, and desperately wicked: who can know it?" Jeremiah 17:9

Technically, we lie for all kinds of selfish reasons. Mostly, people only lie about things that they think matter. Habitual liars lie about everything including things they do not need to lie about.

Nine Reasons People Lie

1. To avoid punishment

"For the wages of sin is death; but the gift of God is eternal life through Jesus Christ our Lord." Romans 6:23a

The number one reason people lie is because they do not want to get in trouble. People do not like consequences. They want to do the crime without doing the time. They do not want penalties or punishment, so they lie to avoid them.

2. They think they can get away with lying

"For there is nothing hidden that will not be disclosed, and nothing concealed that will not be known or brought out into the open." Luke 8:17 NIV

People are so blinded by deceit they actually believe they can lie about something and get away with it. Even if man does not find out, God always knows the truth.

3. They want promotion and rewards

"The labour of the righteous tendeth to life: the fruit of the wicked to sin." Proverbs 10:16

Whatever you compromise to keep you will eventually lose. Even if you obtain a promotion or gain a reward through deception it will only be temporary. Lasting rewards come out of truth, not lies.

4. To avoid embarrassment or shame

"Holding fast the faithful word as he hath been taught, that he may be able by sound doctrine both to exhort and to convince the gainsayers." Titus 1:9

In order to avoid shame and embarrassment from our actions we lie to others about our behaviors. God can use our shame and embarrassment to convict us and call us back to Him.

5. To prevent hurting others

Choosing rather to suffer affliction with the people of God, than to enjoy the pleasures of sin for a season;" Hebrews 11:25

We forget sin hurts us, but it also hurts others as well. There is always collateral damage with sin. Sin will bring pleasure for a season, but when that season ends, it will lead to destruction. Do not lie to yourself and walk in self-righteousness by acting as if you are protecting others from hurt by lying about the truth.

6. To get sympathy from others

"Rejoice with them that do rejoice, and weep with them that weep." Romans 12:15

Sometimes people are so warped that they feel the only way they can get sympathy and compassion from others is by lying. They exaggerate their condition, so they can receive comfort. They are so desperate for love that they lie about their situation even if it means they receive false compassion.

7. To maintain privacy

"I do not understand what I do. For what I want to do I do not do, but what I hate I do." Romans 7:15 NIV

People lie to maintain their privacy not only because they are discreet, but they cannot stand nosey people. However, there is no right reason to do the wrong thing. You can respectfully decline to answer so you do not participate in a lie when your privacy is being invaded.

There is no right reason to do the wrong thing

8. It is a bad habit

"And be not conformed to this world: but be ye transformed by the renewing of your mind, that ye may prove what is that good, and acceptable, and perfect, will of God." Romans 12:2

Bad habits must be renounced and replaced with good habits for transformation to take place in our hearts. Using the excuse that lying is just some bad habit minimizes the importance of walking in the truth.

9. Enjoy risky behavior

"And even as they did not like to retain God in their knowledge, God gave them over to a reprobate mind, to do those things which are not convenient;" Romans 1:28

Some people lie because they are addicted to bad and risky behavior. They enjoy the thrill of doing wrong and getting away with it. Lying about things because they enjoy the thrill of wrongdoing is not just dishonest, it is dysfunctional and deadly.

There is no such thing as a little lie or a big lie any more than there are white lies or black lies.

Lies are lies. For whatever reason we lie, there is no good excuse. Evaluate yourself to check the motivation as to the reason you lie about things to yourself and to other people. It is my prayer that when you truly judge yourself, you will make the decision not to lie anymore, and never excuse away the importance of telling the truth.

CHAPTER 3
The Lies About Truth

Everyone and everything can be lied about, even the truth. The Bible says the ultimate goal of the devil is to keep us separated from God and the best way he does that is by lying about the truth.

Truth can be:

1. Distorted

    "And now, behold, I know that ye all, among whom I have gone preaching the kingdom of God, shall see my face no more. ^{26} Wherefore I take you to record this day, that I am pure from the blood of all men. ^{27} For I have not shunned to declare unto you all the counsel of God. ^{28} Take heed therefore unto yourselves, and to all the flock, over the which the Holy Ghost hath made you overseers, to feed the church of God, which he hath purchased with his own blood. ^{29} For I know this, that after my departing shall grievous wolves enter in among you, not sparing the flock. ^{30} Also of your own selves shall men arise, speaking perverse things, to draw away disciples after them. ^{31} Therefore watch, and remember, that by

the space of three years I ceased not to warn every one night and day with tears." Acts 20:25-31

2. Suppressed

"For the wrath of God is revealed from heaven against all ungodliness and unrighteousness of men, who hold the truth in unrighteousness; [19] *Because that which may be known of God is manifest in them; for God hath shewed it unto them.* [20] *For the invisible things of him from the creation of the world are clearly seen, being understood by the things that are made, even his eternal power and Godhead; so that they are without excuse:"* Romans 1:18-20

3. Rejected

"But after thy hardness and impenitent heart treasurest up unto thyself wrath against the day of wrath and revelation of the righteous judgment of God; [6] *Who will render to every man according to his deeds:* [7] *To them who by patient continuance in well doing seek for glory and honour and immortality, eternal life:* [8] *But unto them that are contentious, and*

do not obey the truth, but obey unrighteousness, indignation and wrath, [9] Tribulation and anguish, upon every soul of man that doeth evil, of the Jew first, and also of the Gentile; [10] But glory, honour, and peace, to every man that worketh good, to the Jew first, and also to the Gentile: [11] For there is no respect of persons with God." Romans 2:5-11

4. Refused

"And with all deceivableness of unrighteousness in them that perish; because they received not the love of the truth, that they might be saved" 2 Thessalonians 2:10

5. Denied

"That they all might be damned who believed not the truth, but had pleasure in unrighteousness." 2 Thessalonians 2:12

Because the devil is such a good liar, he wants to attack Christians to get us to doubt God by questioning the truth. If the enemy gets us to question the truth, he gets us to question God.

---

*If the enemy gets us
to question the truth,
he gets us to
question God*

Eight Great Lies of the Devil

1. The devil wants us to assume our problems do not have solutions.

"When Jesus then lifted up his eyes, and saw a great company come unto him, he saith unto Philip, Whence shall we buy bread, that these may eat? ⁶ And this he said to prove him: for he himself knew what he would do. ⁷ Philip answered him, Two hundred pennyworth of bread is not sufficient for them, that every one of them may take a little." John 6:5-7

Philip was a great disciple but when he assessed the cost of the problem, he assumed no solution was possible. Up to 15,000 people needed to be fed with only 200 pennyworths of bread. Two hundred pennyworth was between 30-35 dollars of bread or 300 dollars in today's monetary system. Three hundred dollars will not feed 15,000 people. When Philip did the calculation, he realized it was not going to happen. What he failed to realize is that with man it is impossible, but with God all things are possible. Do not allow the devil to convince you that you are an exception to the rule and that your problem is so difficult that God does not have a solution.

2. The devil tells us that life should be fair.

"That ye may be the children of your Father which is in heaven: for he maketh his sun to rise on the evil and on the good, and sendeth rain on the just and on the unjust." Matthew 5:45

There are approximately 31,102 scriptures in the Bible and not one promises us that life will be fair. Christians are subject to experiencing tragedy and triumph in life just like everyone else. The only difference is not in the situations we face, but in the way we face the situations. Having God in our hearts does not exempt us from being subject to the natural laws of this world. It does not keep us from experiencing hurt.

3. The devil tells us we married the wrong person.

"What therefore God hath joined together, let not man put asunder." Mark 10:9

The devil is a liar!! He wants to destroy marriages and families. In 1 Corinthians 7:17-24, the Corinthians thought that after salvation, if their spouse did not get saved, they were free to divorce them and get a new spouse. The devil tried to convince them that they were with the wrong person. Paul was telling them that when you get saved, it is important to be a Christian where you are at. Just because God changes your heart, it does not mean you can change your spouse. If you get saved before your spouse, it is important to stay faithful, and allow your example to eventually lead them to Christ.

4. The devil wants you to believe God does not care about you.

"Casting all your care upon him; for he careth for you." 1 Peter 5:7

Any parent understands the unconditional love all parents have for their children. We love our children and do not want them to hurt as God loves us and does not want us to hurt. God always cares about us and what we are going through. God is not some cold-blooded deity who wants us to suffer. God loves and cares for His children.

5. The devil tells us if it feels good, do it.

"And be not conformed to this world: but be ye transformed by the renewing of your mind, that ye may prove what is that good, and acceptable, and perfect, will of God." Romans 12:2

We may be in the world, but we are not of the world. We must be careful not to allow our flesh to rule the day and cause us to believe this lie of the devil. We are not called to feed our flesh but to deny our flesh.

6. The devil tells us life should be easy.

"In the sweat of thy face shalt thou eat bread, till thou return unto the ground; for out of it wast thou taken: for dust thou art, and unto dust shalt thou return." Genesis 3:19

Work is not a curse. It is a cure for boredom and a way to provide good things for our lives. However, work is one reason life is not always easy. Jesus promised we would have stress and tribulation in life. He never promised us a Disneyland or *Fantasy Island* experience. Life is not easy, but Christ can make it easier.

7. The devil wants us to assume the worst in people.

"If thou shalt hear say in one of thy cities, which the Lord thy God hath given thee to dwell there, saying, [13] Certain men, the children of Belial, are gone out from among you, and have withdrawn the inhabitants of their city, saying, Let us go and serve other gods, which ye have not known; [14] Then shalt thou enquire, and make search, and ask diligently; and, behold, if it be truth, and the thing certain, that such abomination is wrought among you; [15] Thou shalt surely smite the inhabitants of that city with the edge of the sword, destroying it utterly, and all that is therein, and the cattle thereof, with the edge of the sword." Deuteronomy 13:12-15

God established a principle in the scripture so people would not act on a rumor and start a war. God told them that there are always two sides to every story so check the facts before taking action. The devil wants you to believe that talking to a person will not do any good. In Numbers 32, representatives of three tribes did not explain themselves clearly and Moses jumped to conclusions and assumed they had selfish motives trying to avoid helping fight for the Promised Land. In reality, they were willing to fight, but they wanted assurances for the safety of their wives and children. In Joshua 22:11-34, three tribes built an altar at the Jordan River. Joshua thought they were starting their own religion but instead of starting a civil war and assuming he was right, Joshua went to them and asked for clarification. The tribes were not building an altar to a separate God but to the same God. Do not assume the worst in people because you could be believing a lie. Assumption is at least a cousin to a lie, so always ask when you do not understand; never assume.

8. The devil wants to keep you in fear of sharing the gospel.

> *"How then shall they call on him in whom they have not believed? and how shall they believe in him of whom they have not heard? and how shall they hear without a preacher? And how shall they preach, except they be sent? as it is written, How beautiful are the feet of them that preach the gospel of peace, and bring glad tidings of good things!" Romans 10:14-15*

Jesus' last command to the church was for us to preach the gospel or give news to the world. The devil wants us to be intimidated by others to the point we feel fear to share the good news of Christ with those who are not saved. We are commanded to share our testimony in hopes that the goodness of God will lead others to salvation. Yes, people might reject your invitation, but they are rejecting God not you. Instead of being negative thinking all will reject the gospel, be a little positive and believe that some might receive the gospel as well.

The devil's job is to lie about the truth. He wants to twist the truth or provide half-truths that lead us to be deceived. Our job is different. We combat all lies and half-truths with the absolute Word of God.

A Christian's Three-Fold Job

1. Comprehend the Truth
2. Conform to the Truth
3. Communicate the Truth

We have to understand the ways of God to the point we apply what we know. We live out all truth so not just our words, but our actions communicate a message to others that truth is our compass. Truth will lead and guide us away from the lies of the enemy and into the freedom that God promises those who walk in the knowledge of the truth of the Word of God.

"And ye shall know the truth, and the truth shall make you free." John 8:32

CHAPTER 4
THE TRUTH ABOUT TRUTH

Truth in many ways can be defined as the opposite of falsehood, but it is also described as verifiable facts. You cannot have truth without facts that can be verified. All of us must have an inner truth that is sustained by a foundation of facts. You are not a car because you live in a garage any more than you are a Christian because you go to church. There has to be proof of your claims of truth. You can identify or claim to be anything, but where is the proof? Truth for a Christian is established by understanding four distinct criteria.

Absolute Truth is Defined in Four Ways

1. God's Laws

   "Thy righteousness is an everlasting righteousness, and thy law is the truth."
   Psalm 119:142

   God's laws are God's commands. Not just the Ten Commandments in Old Testament but hundreds of commands given throughout scripture. One way to always identify truth is to use the commandments of God to be your dictionary.

2. God's Ways

"Teach me thy way, O Lord; I will walk in thy truth: unite my heart to fear thy name." Psalm 86:11

Understanding God's ways is understanding God's nature. God's nature is who He is, not just what He does. God does not give truth, He is truth. God is predictable in His behavior but in unpredictable ways. In other words, God does miracles, but He can do miracles in different ways. People change but God never does. What God was is what God will always be – truth.

3. God's Son

"If so be that ye have heard him, and have been taught by him, as the truth is in Jesus:" Ephesians 4:21

God's son is Jesus Christ. One of His names is truth. If you want absolute truth, it can only be found in Jesus. Jesus was true to the Father, true to the people in the New Testament, and true to Himself. To know Jesus is to know truth.

4. God's Word

"And now, O Lord God, thou art that God, and thy words be true, and thou hast promised this goodness unto thy servant:"
2 Samuel 7:28

God's Word is the Bible. The Bible is truth. Any questions that arise in our lives must be answered by the scriptures. Heaven and earth will pass away, but God's Word will remain. People have tried to burn the Word, blame the Word, and even ban the Word, but the Word still stands as the only absolute truth we can truly trust in.

Our truth must always be established upon the firm foundation of the Word of God.

"Therefore whosoever heareth these sayings of mine, and doeth them, I will liken him unto a wise man, which built his house upon a rock: [25]And the rain descended, and the floods came, and the winds blew, and beat upon that house; and it fell not: for it was founded upon a rock. [26]And every one that heareth these sayings of mine, and doeth them not, shall be likened unto a foolish man, which built his house upon the sand: [27]And the rain descended, and the floods came, and

the winds blew, and beat upon that house; and it fell: and great was the fall of it." Matthew 7:24-27

No good thing can happen without Jesus and the truth of His Word being our firm foundation. There are many other blessings we cannot receive from God until we establish Jesus as our truth.

Ten Rewards that Only Truth Releases

1. Truth releases the reward of wisdom.

    "Behold, thou desirest truth in the inward parts: and in the hidden part thou shalt make me to know wisdom." Psalm 51:6

    No truth, No wisdom.

2. Truth releases the reward of a strong relationship.

    "Lord, who shall abide in thy tabernacle? who shall dwell in thy holy hill? He that walketh uprightly, and worketh righteousness, and speaketh the truth in his heart." Psalm 15:1-2

    Relationships will not last unless they are built on truth.

3. Truth releases the reward of worship.

"God is a Spirit: and they that worship him must worship him in spirit and in truth." John 4:24

Truth and worship are always connected.

4. Truth releases the reward of faithfulness.

"All the paths of the Lord are mercy and truth unto such as keep his covenant and his testimonies." Psalm 25:10

Truthful people are faithful people.

5. Truth releases the reward of freedom.

"And ye shall know the truth, and the truth shall make you free." John 8:32

It is not just any truth that sets us free but the knowledge of the truth of the Word of God.

6. Truth releases the reward of victory over the devil.

"Stand therefore, having your loins girt about with truth, and having on the breastplate of righteousness;" Ephesians 6:14

Putting on the armor of God begins and achieving victory begins with walking in truth.

Deception is at its best when it includes partial truth

7. Truth releases the reward of love.

*"Seeing ye have purified your souls in
obeying the truth through the Spirit unto
unfeigned love of the brethren, see that
ye love one another with a pure heart
fervently:" 1 Peter 1:22*

It is hard to love unless truth leads the way.

8. Truth releases the reward of holiness.

*"By mercy and truth iniquity is purged:
and by the fear of the Lord men depart
from evil." Proverbs 16:6*

You are only as sick as your secrets. You
cannot be purged of evil until you accept and
apply the truth of God to your life.

9. Truth releases the reward of discernment.

*"Even the Spirit of truth; whom the world
cannot receive, because it seeth him not,
neither knoweth him: but ye know him; for
he dwelleth with you, and shall be in you."
John 14:17*

Discernment is a gift given to those who
pursue the truth of God.

10. Truth releases the reward of sanctification.

"Sanctify them through thy truth: thy word is truth." John 17:17

Truth sanctifies and separates us for service in the kingdom of God.

Seeking truth is not optional. When we understand how to obtain truth and embrace the rewards of truth, we will delight in truth even more than we already do. All the facts you need to support absolute truth can be found in the Word of God. The truth of the Word of God has the power to:

- Reveal
- Restore
- Reproduce
- Revive
- Reward
- Repent

Tap into the truth of the Word of God and tap into the power of God. Truth releases gifts and blessings that cannot be released any other way. Blessing always comes as a result of walking in truth.

CHAPTER 5
THE LIE ABOUT LIES

The lie about lies is that you convince yourself that you are actually helping someone by not telling them the truth, and that there are no consequences that are attached to lying. The truth is when people lie it is a great act of selfishness and greed. It is for you, not them. There are blessings attached to our obedience and curses or consequences attached to our disobedience. A consequence is a negative effect that is produced from bad behavior or actions. Lying is a sin and will bring personal consequences and curses upon our lives.

"And thou shalt speak unto the children of Israel, saying, Whosoever curseth his God shall bear his sin." Leviticus 24:15

"The Lord is longsuffering, and of great mercy, forgiving iniquity and transgression, and by no means clearing the guilty, visiting the iniquity of the fathers upon the children unto the third and fourth generation." Numbers 14:18

"For the work of a man shall he render unto him, and cause every man to find according to his ways." Job 34:11

Biblical Examples of Consequences

- Adam and Eve's sin cost them the garden that God created for them.
- Cain's murder of his brother caused him to be isolated and separated.
- Sarah's lack of faith produced an illegitimate child.
- Moses' anger and temper cost him the Promise Land.
- Miriam's racism caused leprosy to fill her body.
- Samson's lust cost him his life.
- David's adultery and murder caused a disconnection from God.
- Solomon's defiance against God's laws of monogamy cost him his happiness.
- Noah's drunkenness caused him to lower the standard.
- Judas' betrayal of Jesus caused mental illness.
- The prodigal son's decision caused him to eat and sleep with the pigs.

No one is exempt or immune to personal consequences that go along with sin. The lie about lies is that the devil tells us that you will not be caught or that you are doing it to protect others. He tells you that you are the exception to the rule. The devil convinces us to continually engage in behavior that becomes worse and worse without considering the cost of our actions. There have been and will always be penalties attached to our behavior. When I was a kid, I loved the sitcom, Baretta, which had a song at the beginning of the show that said, "Don't do the crime if you can't do the time." I love it. It was a catchy phrase that in many ways caused me to be conscious of the consequences of sin before committing the act of sin. You know you are in the flesh and partaking of sin when you avoid being aware of the consequences that sin will bring into your life.

Sixteen Consequences of Lying

1. You lose the trust of people.

   "Then said the prophet Jeremiah unto Hananiah the prophet, Hear now, Hananiah; The Lord hath not sent thee; but thou makest this people to trust in a lie." Jeremiah 28:15

2. You lose your value to others.

   "And the Lord spake unto Moses and Aaron, Because ye believed me not, to sanctify me in the eyes of the children of Israel, therefore ye shall not bring this congregation into the land which I have given them." Numbers 20:12

3. You hurt others.

"A lying tongue hateth those that are afflicted by it; and a flattering mouth worketh ruin." Proverbs 26:28

4. You feel uneasy thinking you could be caught in your lie.

"And hereby we know that we are of the truth, and shall assure our hearts before him. For if our heart condemn us, God is greater than our heart, and knoweth all things. Beloved, if our heart condemn us not, then have we confidence toward God." 1 John 3:19-21

5. You situate yourself in a place where you could reap what you sow.

"Be not deceived; God is not mocked: for whatsoever a man soweth, that shall he also reap." Galatians 6:7

6. You cannot experience joy.

"Restore unto me the joy of thy salvation; and uphold me with thy free spirit." Psalm 51:12

7. You have insecurity in yourself, and you distrust others.

"But if ye have bitter envying and strife in your hearts, glory not, and lie not against the truth." James 3:14

8. You walk in fear, not faith.

"The wicked flee when no man pursueth: but the righteous are bold as a lion." Proverbs 28:1

9. You have an aura of suspicion surrounding you.

"When I kept silence, my bones waxed old through my roaring all the day long. For day and night thy hand was heavy upon me: my moisture is turned into the drought of summer. Selah. I acknowledge my sin unto thee, and mine iniquity have I not hid. I said, I will confess my transgressions unto the Lord; and thou forgavest the iniquity of my sin. Selah." Psalm 32:3-5

*Lying will take you
where you do not
want to go, cost you
more than you are
willing to pay, and
keep you there
longer than you
want to stay*

10. You pass a lying spirit to your children.

"The Lord is longsuffering, and of great mercy, forgiving iniquity and transgression, and by no means clearing the guilty, visiting the iniquity of the fathers upon the children unto the third and fourth generation." Numbers 14:18

11. You cannot separate fantasy from reality.

"But refuse profane and old wives' fables, and exercise thyself rather unto godliness." 1 Timothy 4:7

12. You suffer from sickness and cannot walk in health.

"There is no soundness in my flesh because of thine anger; neither is there any rest in my bones because of my sin." Psalm 38:3

13. You have to tell more lies to cover up your original lie.

"Woe to the rebellious children, saith the Lord, that take counsel, but not of me; and that cover with a covering, but not of my

spirit, that they may add sin to sin:"
Isaiah 30:1

14. You destroy God-given relationships.

"A man that hath friends must shew himself friendly: and there is a friend that sticketh closer than a brother." Proverbs 18:24

15. You end up in a devil's hell.

"But the fearful, and unbelieving, and the abominable, and murderers, and whoremongers, and sorcerers, and idolaters, and all liars, shall have their part in the lake which burneth with fire and brimstone: which is the second death." Revelation 21:8

16. You separate yourself from God.

"But your iniquities have separated between you and your God, and your sins have hid his face from you, that he will not hear." Isaiah 59:2

Do not buy into or believe the lie about lies. Lying is dangerous, destructive, and deadly. Lying will take you where you do not want to go and cost you more than you are willing to pay, and keep you there longer than you want to stay.

CHAPTER 6
THE TRUTH ABOUT GOD

All my life I have heard God can do anything. I still believe that, but my belief system has refined to also add there are some things God cannot do. I am not trying to be coy or disrespectful, but I have complied a list of things God cannot do.

20 Things God Cannot Do!!!

1. God cannot lie.

   "That by two immutable things, in which it was impossible for God to lie, we might have a strong consolation, who have fled for refuge to lay hold upon the hope set before us:" Hebrews 6:18

2. God cannot be given an unsolvable problem.

   "But Jesus beheld them, and said unto them, With men this is impossible; but with God all things are possible." Matthew 19:26

3. God cannot leave you alone.

   "And, behold, I am with thee, and will keep thee in all places whither thou goest,

and will bring thee again into this land; for I will not leave thee, until I have done that which I have spoken to thee of." Genesis 28:15

4. God cannot stop loving you.

   "The Lord hath appeared of old unto me, saying, Yea, I have loved thee with an everlasting love: therefore with lovingkindness have I drawn thee." Jeremiah 31:3

5. God cannot stand sin.

   "But your iniquities have separated between you and your God, and your sins have hid his face from you, that he will not hear." Isaiah 59:2

6. God cannot leave a work He started unfinished.

   "Being confident of this very thing, that he which hath begun a good work in you will perform it until the day of Jesus Christ:" Philippians 1:6

7. God cannot be praised enough.

"Praise ye the Lord. Praise God in his sanctuary: praise him in the firmament of his power. ²Praise him for his mighty acts: praise him according to his excellent greatness.³Praise him with the sound of the trumpet: praise him with the psaltery and harp.⁴Praise him with the timbrel and dance: praise him with stringed instruments and organs.5 Praise him upon the loud cymbals: praise him upon the high sounding cymbals." Psalm 150

8. God cannot fail.

"Be strong and of a good courage, fear not, nor be afraid of them: for the Lord thy God, he it is that doth go with thee; he will not fail thee, nor forsake thee." Deuteronomy 31:6

9. God cannot be blamed if we do not make it to heaven.

"How shall we escape, if we neglect so great salvation; which at the first began to be spoken by the Lord, and was confirmed unto us by them that heard him;" Hebrews 2:3

Truth has been

created by God but

lies have been

invented by the devil

---

10. God cannot be superseded.

"And he is before all things, and by him all things consist." Colossians 1:17

11. God cannot accept less than our best.

"I beseech you therefore, brethren, by the mercies of God, that ye present your bodies a living sacrifice, holy, acceptable unto God, which is your reasonable service." Romans 12:1

12. God cannot be figured out.

"As thou knowest not what is the way of the spirit, nor how the bones do grow in the womb of her that is with child: even so thou knowest not the works of God who maketh all." Ecclesiastes 11:5

13. God cannot be unfaithful.

"They are new every morning: great is thy faithfulness." Lamentations 3:23

14. God cannot have burdens that are heavy.

"For my yoke is easy, and my burden is light." Matthew 11:30

15. God cannot accept doubt.

"But without faith it is impossible to please him: for he that cometh to God must believe that he is, and that he is a rewarder of them that diligently seek him." Hebrews 11:6

16. God cannot give His children bad gifts.

"If ye then, being evil, know how to give good gifts unto your children, how much more shall your Father which is in heaven give good things to them that ask him?" Matthew 7:11

17. God cannot grow weary.

"Hast thou not known? hast thou not heard, that the everlasting God, the Lord, the Creator of the ends of the earth, fainteth not, neither is weary? there is no searching of his understanding." Isaiah 40:28

18. God cannot have a problem that is too difficult.

"Ah Lord God! behold, thou hast made the heaven and the earth by thy great

power and stretched out arm, and there is nothing too hard for thee:" Jeremiah 32:17

19. God cannot be lost.

"And ye shall seek me, and find me, when ye shall search for me with all your heart." Jeremiah 29:13

20. God cannot hate.

"He that loveth not knoweth not God; for God is love." 1 John 4:8

The reason I put this chapter in the book is because the devil is such a liar. He will attempt to tell you bad things about God. These scriptures will help you to combat all the lies the devil tries to tell you about God. It will also help you to understand the truth about God that the devil is always wanting to cover up, so you will not walk in your freedom. Jesus used the truth of the Word of God to overcome the devil, and we must do the same.

CHAPTER 7
BIBLICAL FACTS ABOUT TRUTH AND LIES

Just as light always penetrates darkness, truth always overcomes lies. The best truth to use to achieve victory in this world is Jesus. Jesus is truth, Jesus is the Word. John 1:1 declares, *"In the beginning was the Word, and the Word was with God, and the Word was God."*
In case I have not been clear enough up to this point, here are some scriptures that expose the impact of lying and reveal the importance of always walking in truth.

Twelve Facts About Lying

1. Lying is something God hates with a passion.

   "Lying lips are abomination to the Lord: but they that deal truly are his delight."
   Proverbs 12:22

2. Liars will not escape punishment and penalty.

   "A false witness shall not be unpunished, and he that speaketh lies shall perish."
   Proverbs 19:9

3. Lying keeps you separated from God's presence.

   "No one who practices deceit will dwell in my house; no one who speaks falsely will stand in my presence." Psalm 101:7 NIV

4. All lies and secrets will ultimately be exposed.

   "For nothing is secret, that shall not be made manifest; neither any thing hid, that shall not be known and come abroad." Luke 8:17

5. Liars are unfaithful people.

   "He that saith, I know him, and keepeth not his commandments, is a liar, and the truth is not in him." 1 John 2:4

6. Lying can only gain you a temporary advantage.

   "The getting of treasures by a lying tongue is a vanity tossed to and fro of them that seek death." Proverbs 21:6

7. Lying is birthed in jealousy and self-ambition.

   "But if ye have bitter envying and strife in your hearts, glory not, and lie not against the truth." James 3:14

8. Lying is a prerequisite to involvement in other sins.

   "By swearing, and lying, and killing, and stealing, and committing adultery, they break out, and blood toucheth blood." Hosea 4:2

9. A liar's fate is unhappiness and premature death.

   "What man is he that desireth life, and loveth many days, that he may see good? Keep thy tongue from evil, and thy lips from speaking guile." Psalm 34:12-13

10. Liars have an enemy in God.

   "Behold, I am against them that prophesy false dreams, saith the Lord, and do tell them, and cause my people to err by their lies, and by their lightness; yet I sent them

not, nor commanded them: therefore they shall not profit this people at all, saith the Lord." Jeremiah 23:32

11. Lying is a sin.

"If we say that we have no sin, we deceive ourselves, and the truth is not in us." 1 John 1:8

12. Lying is impossible for God to do.

"That by two immutable things, in which it was impossible for God to lie, we might have a strong consolation, who have fled for refuge to lay hold upon the hope set before us:" Hebrews 6:18

Twelve Facts About the Truth

1. Truth should always be spoken in love.

"But speaking the truth in love, may grow up into him in all things, which is the head, even Christ:" Ephesians 4:15

*The truth may hurt
for a little while, but
a lie hurts forever*

2. Truth releases the favor of God.

"The lips of the righteous know what is acceptable: but the mouth of the wicked speaketh frowardness." Proverbs 10:32

3. Truth from God's Word gives true freedom from bondage.

"And ye shall know the truth, and the truth shall make you free." John 8:32

4. Truth is our armor to help us to defend against the enemy's attacks.

"Stand therefore, having your loins girt about with truth, and having on the breastplate of righteousness;" Ephesians 6:14

5. Truth ushers in the presence of God into our lives.

"Lord, who shall abide in thy tabernacle? who shall dwell in thy holy hill? He that walketh uprightly, and worketh righteousness, and speaketh the truth in his heart." Psalm 15:1-2

6. Truth is eternal.

"For the truth's sake, which dwelleth in us, and shall be with us for ever." 2 John 1:2

7. Truth is short and direct.

"But above all things, my brethren, swear not, neither by heaven, neither by the earth, neither by any other oath: but let your yea be yea; and your nay, nay; lest ye fall into condemnation." James 5:12

8. Truth is a characteristic of love.

"Charity suffereth long, and is kind; charity envieth not; charity vaunteth not itself, is not puffed up, Doth not behave itself unseemly, seeketh not her own, is not easily provoked, thinketh no evil; Rejoiceth not in iniquity, but rejoiceth in the truth;" 1 Corinthians 13:4-6

9. Truth takes place in your mind before it manifests in your life.

"Finally, brethren, whatsoever things are true, whatsoever things are honest, whatsoever things are just, whatsoever

things are pure, whatsoever things are lovely, whatsoever things are of good report; if there be any virtue, and if there be any praise, think on these things." Philippians 4:8

10. Truth is the light that leads us out of darkness.

"O send out thy light and thy truth: let them lead me; let them bring me unto thy holy hill, and to thy tabernacles." Psalm 43:3

11. Truth is a trait that others can discern or recognize in us.

"And the woman said to Elijah, Now by this I know that thou art a man of God, and that the word of the Lord in thy mouth is truth." 1 Kings 17:24

12. Truth is what separates the "saints" from the "aint's".

"Sanctify them through thy truth: thy word is truth." John 17:17

Truth defeats deceit every time we choose to use the Word. The truth of God's Word is what separates the flesh from the spirit, so we can be more like God and less like us.

CHAPTER 8
QUOTES, QUICKS, & QUIPS

In this chapter, I have compiled some of my favorite quotes, quicks, and quips. These are a collection of over thirty years of preaching and reading. Some are my own sayings, and some I have been quoting for so long I do not remember where they came from. I have made reference to the material if the source is known. I hope you enjoy these as much as I have over the years.

QUOTES

A quote is mostly a one sentence statement that is worth repeating that sums up a subject or theme. In a spiritual sense, it is a sermon sentence.

- "People who do what is right never fear the truth."

- "The truth never lies."

- "The truth only hurts when you want to believe a lie."

- "A half-truth is a whole lie."

- "It is way easier to remember the truth than it is a lie."

- "Honesty is the first chapter in the book of wisdom." – Thomas Jefferson

- "Opinion is not truth."

- "Truth has been created by God but lies are invented by the devil."

- "Repetition does not transform a lie into a truth." - Franklin D. Roosevelt

- "Deception is at its best when it includes partial truth."

- "Exaggeration is at least a cousin of a lie."

- "The truth can walk around naked; the lie has to be clothed." - A Yiddish proverb

- "Truth gives a short answer, while the lie usually babbles." - German proverb

- "Telling the truth and making someone cry is better than telling a lie and making someone smile."

- "If you stop telling lies about me, I'll stop telling the truth about you."

- "Dishonesty is disrespect."

- "To sum everything up, the truth about lies is that the truth never lies, and the lie about the truth is that lies never tell the truth."

- "Tell the truth, or someone will tell it for you."

- "You cannot argue with people who believe their own lies."

- "The truth may hurt for a little while, but a lie hurts forever."

- "Better to get hurt by the truth than be comforted with a lie."

- "The longer the explanation, the bigger the lie."

- "What is worse - people who lie or the people who think I am stupid enough to believe their lies?"

- "No man has a good enough memory to be a successful liar." - Abraham Lincoln

- "I'm sorry if you don't like my honesty, but to be fair, I don't like your lies."

- "It only takes one lie to question all your so-called truth."

- "The first lie the devil will tell you will be the last truth God speaks."

QUICKS

A quick is defined as an odd or interesting fact that is short and to the point.

- According to a study done by the University of Notre Dame, telling the truth can improve your health. The study found that telling fewer lies per week improved both mental health and physical health.

- According to a study published in the *Journal of Basic and Applied Social Psychology*, 60% of people lie at least once in every ten-minute conversation.

- People are not very accurate at telling when someone is lying to them. Studies show that people can tell when someone is lying about as accurately as they can call a coin toss— about 52% of the time.

- The commonly held belief that people fidget or look away when they lie… isn't true. We've been lied to about lying.

- There is computer software that can tell when someone is lying better than people can. It's called the Linguistic Inquiry and Word Count, and it catches liars 67% of the time rather than the 52% that people do. It does this by asking a person to write a sample into the computer and then it looks for the components like first person pronouns, negative words, and exclusionary words.

- We lie the most when we are teenagers— between the ages of 13-17. The ages in which we lie the least? When we are six through eight years old.

- Men and women both tell the same amount of lies, though what they lie about tends to differ. Women tend to lie to make other people feel better, and men tend to lie to make themselves look better.

- Pinocchio was the first animated film to win an Academy Award in a competitive category in 1939. Pinocchio cost $2.8 million to make and was one of the most expensive films produced at that time. It is about a wooden puppet who wanted to be a real boy who when he told lies, his nose would grow.

- There have been hundreds of Hollywood movies made around the theme of lying. Here are a few:

    1. *Liar Liar* with Jim Carrey
    2. *The Proposal* with Ryan Reynolds and Sandra Bullock
    3. *Tootsie* with Dustin Hoffman
    4. *True Lies* with Arnold Schwarzenegger
    5. *Sex, Lies, and Videotape* with Andie MacDowell and James Spader

- Lying is mentioned approximately 170 times in the Bible, while truth is mentioned approximately 250 times.

- The nicotine lie that came from the cigarette companies in the 1990's was that cigarette smoking was no more 'addictive' than coffee, tea, or Twinkies.

- At the 1919 World Series, eight Chicago White Sox baseball players intentionally lost against the Cincinnati Reds in exchange for a gambling bribe of $100,000. It became known as the Black Sox Baseball Cheating Scandal.

QUIPS

A quip is defined as a clever or funny remark. A witty observation, or a joke.

A minister told his congregation, "Next week I plan to preach about the sin of lying. To help you understand my sermon, I want you all to read Mark 17."

The following Sunday, as he prepared to deliver his sermon, the minister asked for a show of hands. He wanted to know how many had read Mark 17. Every hand went up. The minister smiled and said, "Mark has only sixteen chapters. I will now proceed with my sermon on the sin of lying."

Two boys were arguing in class one day when the teacher walked into the classroom. The teacher asked them, "Why are you arguing?" One of the boys replied, "We found a ten-dollar bill and decided to give it to whoever tells the biggest lie." "You should be ashamed of yourselves," said the teacher. "When I was your age, I didn't even know what a lie was."

The boys gave the ten dollars to the teacher.

One time this kid came back from school and said, "Mom I have one good news and one bad news, which one do you wanna hear first?" And his mom said, "Good news please.' The boy said, "I got 100% on my math test today" and his mom gave him a hug, and the boy said, "Now to the bad news, I lied."

The cheetah had a race with a lion and the cheetah won. The lion was like, "Why you always a cheetah?" The cheetah was like, "Why you always lion (lying)?"

I always want to make reading fun and enjoyable. So, I like adding chapters to my books to make it more interesting. This chapter gives you the one-liners, sermon sentences, uncommon insight, and even jokes to help connect you to the overall themes of the book but also provides clever insight into truth and lies. The message of this book is to avoid lying and embrace the truth.

CHAPTER 9

This is a fun chapter to challenge your biblical knowledge of the scriptures. As a kid in school, I hated all tests and quizzes. However, as an adult I am challenged by opportunities to put my knowledge of the Word of God into effect. I am giving you several true or false questions that must be read carefully to avoid being deceived. I am telling you in advance that there are some trick questions that you will be asked, so read carefully, and use your spiritual discernment and knowledge to answer all questions correctly. The devil must have partial truth to deceive, so hopefully you can use this quiz to refine your skills to be aware of the devil's tactics while at the same time be encouraged that you are being educated in the things of God. Try answering these questions on your own, looking in the Bible, or maybe even Googling the answer to ensure the correctness of your answers.

Bible Test

1. "Jesus wept," the shortest verse in the Bible, is only two words long.

   True or False

2. Abel's sacrifice was rejected by God.

   True or False

3. Lot's wife, Abigail, was turned into a pillar of salt when she looked back upon Sodom and Gomorrah.

   True or False

4. Peter was a fisherman when Jesus called him to be a disciple.

   True or False

5. The disciple, Luke, was a medical doctor.

   True or False

6. The final word in the Christian Bible, according to the KJV, NKJV, and NIV, is "Amen."

   True or False

7. With two loaves and five fish, Jesus fed 5,000 men not including women and children.

   True or False

8. The death of the firstborn was Egypt's final plague.

   True or False

9. Corinthians was one of the seven churches mentioned in the book of Revelation.

   True or False

10. The apostle Paul was a tentmaker.

    True or False

11. During David's reign, Zadok was a priest.

    True or False

12. Ananias and Sapphira were killed for lying about the price of a plot of land they sold.

    True or False

13. Johnathan was one of David's sons.

    True or False

14. On the fourth day of creation, God created birds and fish.

    True or False

15. To be cured of his leprosy, Naaman was instructed to dip himself seven times in the Tigris River.

    True or False

16. Jesus was born in the town of Nazareth.

    True or False

17. Moses fled to Midian after killing an Egyptian.

    True or False

18. Isaac was Abraham's first-born son.

    True or False

19. On his way to Damascus, Paul was converted to Christ.

    True or False

20. Moses led the children of Israel across the Jordan River into the Promised Land.

True of False

21. John the Baptist baptized Jesus.

True or False

22. In Jerusalem, Jesus noticed Zacchaeus climbing a sycamore tree.

True or False

23. When David was thrown into the lion's den, God gave the lion lockjaw.

True or False

24. Israel wandered in the wilderness for forty years.

True or False

25. There were only nine people on Noah's ark.

True or False

26. Paul wrote 12 of the 27 books in the New Testament.

   True or False

27. Saul was Israel's first king.

   True or False

28. Methuselah lived to be 969 years old, according to the Bible.

   True or False

29. Jacob had a coat of many colors.

   True or False

30. In Revelation, Paul wrote a letter to seven churches.

   True or False

*The longer the
explanation, the
bigger the lie*

ANSWERS

Answers to the Test

1. True

2. False

It was Cain's sacrifice that was rejected by God.

3. False

No name was given for lot's wife in the Bible.

4. True

5. True

6. True

7. False

It was five loaves and two fish.

8. True

9. False

10. True

11. True

12. True

13. False

Jonathan was David's closest friend.

14. False

It was on the fifth day that God created birds and fish.

15. False

It was the Jordan river.

16. False

Jesus was born in Bethlehem.

17. True

18. False

Ishmael was Abraham's first son.

19. True

20. False

It was Joshua who led Israel into the Promised Land.

21. True

22. False

Zacchaeus climbed a tree in Jericho.

23. False

Daniel, not David, was thrown into the lion's den.

24. True

25. False

There were eight people on Noah's ark.

26. False

Paul wrote at least 13 New Testament books.

27. True

28. True

29. False

It was Joseph who had a coat of many colors.

30. False

John wrote the letter to the seven churches in Revelation.

So … How did you do? Do not get prideful if you got them all correct, and do not feel like a loser if you got more wrong than what you thought you should have. The whole purpose of this chapter is to show you how subtle deception can be. We must pay attention to every word and think through things carefully and use the Word of God to make the right conclusions. The devil is clever, so we have to walk in the wisdom of God.

If you stop telling

lies about me, I will

stop telling the truth

about you

CONCLUSION

There is a lot to digest in this book, but do not forget that God is the Father of Truth, and the devil is the father of lies. We must stand firm, or we will fall fast. Premeditate truth, and desire to walk in truth. Make a decision to never lie. I want to leave you with a life message that needs to be your vision moving forward. Let this word be your mission from God that you must complete.

Your Three-Fold Mission in Life

1. Learn the Truth

   "Finally, brethren, whatsoever things are true, whatsoever things are honest, whatsoever things are just, whatsoever things are pure, whatsoever things are lovely, whatsoever things are of good report; if there be any virtue, and if there be any praise, think on these things." Philippians 4:8

   Learn the truth by learning the Word. Saturate yourself in the scriptures. It is natural to lie, it is supernatural to learn the truth.

2. Love the Truth

"And with all deceivableness of unrighteousness in them that perish; because they received not the love of the truth, that they might be saved."
2 Thessalonians 2:10

A person is not a liar because they tell lies, they tell lies because they are a liar. You have to hate lying, but you also have to love the truth to experience true freedom. Knowing the truth is loving the truth.

3. Live the Truth

"Wherefore putting away lying, speak every man truth with his neighbour: for we are members one of another."
Ephesians 4:25

Make a decision to live out the truth, not just to be an example for others but to be true to yourself.

I pray this book opens your heart up to walking in integrity by walking in truth. Anyone can be a liar. Anyone can lie. Lying is easy, it takes little to no work. Truth is much harder to obtain but made easier by knowing God and knowing His

Word. Refuse to be a liar and desire to always seek the truth.

Prayer of Truth

Father, in the name of Jesus, I come before you to repent of all my deceitfulness and lies. I want to be honest with God, others, and myself. I want to change to become more like Jesus. I do not want to be someone who flatters others to manipulate them to get something from them. I want to do a better job in speaking life instead of death and never gossip about other people. Help me to mind my own business and use Your Word to test the spirits to see if I am hearing from God, my flesh, or the devil. I want to be balanced and never exaggerate the truth. Deliver me from myself and my selfish ambition that causes me to lie about things that are unnecessary. I always want to learn the truth, love the truth, and live the truth so I am not a hypocrite. Help me to discern the truth about lies and lies about truth. I always want to choose the truth and never reject, refuse, distort, suppress, or deny the truth. Help me to remember if the devil is speaking to me, then he is lying to me to divert me from completing God's perfect will in my life. Enable the truth of God to bring liberty in all areas of bondage and release the blessings that only absolute truth can bring. Let all darkness in my heart be exposed by the light of God's Holy Word. Always remind me that it is impossible for You, Oh God, to lie because Truth is who You are. I renounce and rebuke every lying spirit that is coming against me. Every half-truth and complete lie must bow down to Jesus Christ. I will allow no deceit to occupy space in my heart or mind and no untruthful statement will come out of my mouth. Only truth can exist in my entire being. Truth rules my life in Jesus' name, Amen.

To get daily wisdom nuggets, check out Pastor Bill on social media for the most important minute of your day!

The Minute That Matters

Scan the QR code with your phone, and you will be automatically connected to your choice of social media.